This book
belongs
to

....

A CHILD'S YEAR OF STORIES AND POEMS

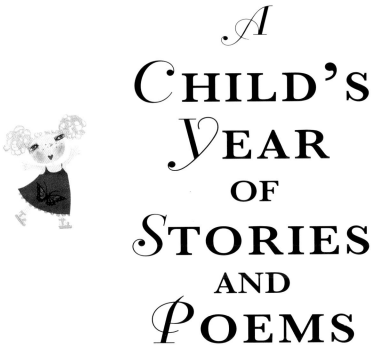

PUFFIN BOOKS

VIKING/PUFFIN

Published by the Penguin Group
Penguin Books Ltd, 27 Wrights Lane, London W8 5TZ, England
Penguin Putnam Inc., 375 Hudson Street, New York, New York 10014, USA
Penguin Books Australia Ltd, Ringwood, Victoria, Australia
Penguin Books Canada Ltd, 10 Alcorn Avenue, Toronto, Ontario, Canada M4V 3B2
Penguin Books (NZ) Ltd, Private Bag 102902, NSMC, Auckland, New Zealand

On the World Wide Web at: www.penguin.com

Penguin Books Ltd, Registered Offices: Harmondsworth, Middlesex, England

First published 2000
1 3 5 7 9 10 8 6 4 2

This collection copyright © Penguin Books Ltd, 2000
'Spring' illustrations copyright © Sheila Moxley, 2000
'Summer' illustrations copyright © Lydia Monks, 2000
'Autumn' illustrations copyright © Ruth Rivers, 2000
'Winter' illustrations copyright © Tom Saeker, 2000
The acknowledgements on pages 8, 38, 68 and 98 constitute an extension of this copyright page

British Library Cataloguing in Publication Data
A CIP catalogue record for this book is available from the British Library

ISBN 0–670–88953–9

CONTENTS

Spring

Summer

Autumn

Winter

Spring

Illustrated by
SHEILA MOXLEY

ACKNOWLEDGEMENTS

The editor and publisher gratefully acknowledges permission to reproduce the following copyright material:

'A Date with Spring' by John Agard from *Get Back, Pimple!* published by Viking Children's Books 1996. Copyright © John Agard, 1996. Reproduced by permission of the Caroline Sheldon Literary Agency on behalf of John Agard.

'Goodbye My Winter Suit' by N. M. Bodecker from *Hurry, Hurry, Mary Dear* published by Orion Children's Books. Copyright © N. M. Bodecker. Reproduced by permission of The Orion Publishing Group Ltd.

'The Spring Rabbit' by Joyce Dunbar from *The Spring Rabbit* published by Andersen Press Ltd 1994. Text copyright © Joyce Dunbar, 1994. Reproduced by permission of Andersen Press Ltd.

'The Fight of the Year' by Roger McGough from *Watchwords* by Roger McGough. Copyright © Roger McGough, 1969. Reproduced by permission of The Peters, Fraser & Dunlop Group Ltd, on behalf of Roger McGough.

'I Planted Some Seeds' by Colin McNaughton from *There's An Awful Lot of Weirdos in our Neighbourhood* published by Walker Books Ltd. Copyright © Colin McNaughton, 1987. Reproduced by permission of Walker Books Ltd, London.

'Spring' by Michelle Magorian from *Orange Paw Marks* published by Viking Children's Books 1989. Copyright © Michelle Magorian, 1989. Reproduced by perminssion of Rogers Coleridge and White Ltd

'First Spring' by Grace Nichols from *Give Yourself a Hug* published by A & C Black 1984. Copyright © Grace Nichols, 1984. Reproduced by permission of Curtis Brown Ltd, London, on behalf of Grace Nichols.

'Carpet of Blue' by Hiawyn Oram from *Out of the Blue* published by Andersen Press Ltd 1992. Copyright © Hiawyn Oram, 1992. Reproduced by permission of Andersen Press Ltd.

'The Magpie's Nest' by Michael Rosen. Text copyright © Michael Rosen, 1972 Reprinted by permission of the author.

'Stocking and Shirt' and 'Cows' by James Reeves from *Complete Poems for Children* by James Reeves, published by Heinemann. Reproduced by permission of Laura Cecil on behalf of the James Reeves Estate.

Every effort has been made to trace copyright holders. The editor and publisher would like to hear from any copyright holders not acknowledged.

First Spring

ou know that winter's almost gone
     when you step outside and feel
the first warm fingers of the sun
touching your back,
like a hesitant friend.

You know that winter's almost gone
when you walk around
and suddenly, in the back garden –
a posse of daffodils
nodding to the earth's sweet hum.

Now you're running out the gate
Now you're running . . . down the pave
There's a shout in your wave
There's a skip in your sing.

It's the first day of spring.

GRACE NICHOLS

9

The Fight of the Year

'And there goes the bell for the third month
and Winter comes out of its corner looking groggy
Spring leads with a left to the head
followed by a sharp right to the body
daffodils
primroses
crocuses
snowdrops
lilacs
violets
pussywillow

Winter can't take much more punishment
and spring shows no signs of tiring
tadpoles
squirrels
baa-lambs
badgers
bunny rabbits
mad march hares
horses and hounds

Spring is merciless
Winter won't go the full twelve rounds
bobtail clouds
scallywag winds
the sun
a pavement artist
in every town

A left to the chin and Winter's down!
tomatoes
radish
cucumber
onions
beetroot
celery
and any
amount
of lettuce
for dinner

Winter's out for the count
Spring is the winner!'

ROGER McGOUGH

11

Goodbye My Winter Suit

Goodbye my winter suit,
    goodbye my hat and boot,
goodbye my ear-protecting muffs,
    and storms that hail and hoot.

Farewell to snow and sleet,
    farewell to cream of wheat,
farewell to ice-removing salt
    and slush around my feet.

Right on! to daffodils,
    right on! to whippoorwills,
right on! to chirp-producing eggs
    and baby birds and quills.

The day is on the wing,
    the kite is on the string,
the sun is where the sun should be —
    it's spring all right! It's Spring!

N. M. Bodecker

Written in March

While resting on the bridge at the foot of Brother's Water

The cock is crowing,
      The stream is flowing,
The small birds twitter,
The lake doth glitter,
The green field sleeps in the sun;
The oldest and youngest
Are at work with the strongest;
The cattle are grazing,
Their heads never raising;
There are forty feeding like one!

Like an army defeated
The snow hath retreated,
And now doth fare ill
On the top of the bare hill;
The plough boy is whooping
                – anon – anon:
There's joy in the mountains;
There's life in the fountains;
Small clouds are sailing,
Blue sky prevailing;
The rain is over and gone!

WILLIAM WORDSWORTH

The Browny Hen

A browny hen sat on her nest
    With a hey-ho for the springtime!
Seven brown eggs 'neath her downy breast,
    With a hey-ho for the springtime!

A browny hen clucks all day from dawn,
    With a hey-ho for the springtime!
She's seven wee chicks as yellow as corn,
    With a hey-ho for the springtime!

IRENE F. FAWSEY

Minnie and Mattie

Minnie and Mattie
   And fat little May
Out in the country,
Spending a day.

Such a bright day,
With the sun glowing,
And the trees half in leaf,
And the grass growing.

Pinky white pigling
Squeals through his snout,
Woolly white lambkin
Frisks all about.

Cluck! Cluck! The nursing hen
Summons her folk,
Ducklings all downy soft,
Yellow as yolk.

Minnie and Mattie
And May carry posies,
Half of sweet violets,
Half of primroses.

Violets and primroses,
Blossoms today
For Minnie and Mattie
And fat little May.

Christina Rossetti

The Magpie's Nest

Michael Rosen

Once a long time ago, when winter was nearly over and spring had nearly begun, all the birds were busy starting to build their nests. There they all were: the robin and the eagle, the seagull, the blackbird, the duck, the owl and the humming bird, all busy. All, that is, except Magpie. And she didn't feel much like working.

It was a nice day and she was out and about looking for scrips and scraps and bibs and bobs for her collection of old junk — her hoard of bits and pieces she had picked up from behind chimneys or from drain-pipes. Pebbles, beads, buttons and the like, anything bright and interesting or unusual, Magpie was sure to collect. Just as she was flying along on the look-out for a new treasure, she caught sight of Sparrow, her mouth full of bits of straw and twigs.

'What are you doing, what are you doing?' said Magpie.

'Building my nest,' said Sparrow, 'like you'll have to soon.'

'Oh yes?' said Magpie.

'Yes,' said Sparrow, 'put that milk-bottle-top down and come over here and watch. First you have to find a twig, and then another twig, another twig, another twig, another twig . . .'

'Don't make me laugh,' said Magpie, 'I know, I know, I know all that,' and off she flew. And as she flew on looking for scrips and scraps and bibs and bobs she came up to Duck who was upside down with her mouth full of mud.

'What are you doing, what are you doing?' said Magpie.

'Building my nest,' said Duck,
'like you'll have to soon.'

'Oh yes?' said Magpie.

'Yes,' said Duck, 'throw away that old
earwig and watch me. After you've
got all your twigs you have to stick
them with mud pats like this –
pat-pat, pat-pat, pat-pat . . .'

'Don't make me laugh,' said
Magpie, 'I know, I know, I know all that,'
and off she flew. And as she flew on looking for scrips and scraps
and bibs and bobs she saw Pigeon with a mouthful of feathers.

'What are you doing, what are you doing?' said Magpie.

'Building my nest,' said Pigeon,
'like you'll have to soon.'

'Oh yes?' said Magpie.

'Yes,' said Pigeon, 'put that bus ticket
down and come over here and learn how.
You have to make yourself warm and
cosy – right? Right. So you dig your

beak into your chest like this – right? And find one of those very soft, fluffy feathers down there and you lay that out very carefully inside your nest to keep it warm and cosy, warm and cosy, warm and cosy . . .'

'Don't make me laugh,' said Magpie, 'I know, I know, I know, I know all that,' and off she flew.

Well, not long after that it was time for Magpie to lay her eggs and she looked out from her perch and saw all the other birds sitting in their well-built, warm, cosy nests, laying their eggs. 'Oh no,' said Magpie, 'I haven't got anywhere to lay mine! I'd better hurry.' And she remembered Sparrow saying something about twigs and Duck about patting them and Pigeon saying something about cosy feathers. So she rushed out and quickly grabbed as many twigs as she could, made a great pile of them, threw a feather on the top – and the milk-bottle top and the earwig and the bus ticket and she *just* had time to sit herself down and lay her eggs.

And if you look at a magpie's nest you'll see it's always a mess. And she ends up throwing her scrips and scraps and bibs and bobs in it too.

I think she likes it like that.

I Planted Some Seeds

I planted some seeds
In my garden today.
They haven't come up yet,
I hope they're okay.

Should I dig them all up,
Take them back to the shop?
Ask for my money back,
Say they're a flop?

Perhaps they were faulty,
Perhaps they were duff,
Maybe they haven't
Been watered enough.

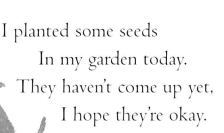

I planted some seeds
In my garden today.
They haven't come up yet,
I hope they're okay.

Colin McNaughton

19

I'm Glad

I'm glad the sky is painted blue,
And earth is painted green,
With such a lot of nice fresh air
All sandwiched in between.

ANONYMOUS

The Echoing Green

The sun does arise,
And make happy the skies;
The merry bells ring
To welcome the spring;
The skylark and thrush,
The birds of the bush,
Sing louder around
To the bells' cheerful sound,
While our sports shall be seen
On the Echoing Green.

WILLIAM BLAKE

Sweet Spring

The trees are clouds of coconut ice,
　　The air is peppermint bright.
The fields are terrines of browns and greens
　　In the morning's milky light.

The hedges and paths are spread with sweets,
　　Primroses preserved in dew.
The spider's run is sugar spun
　　As a master chef might do.

The drifts of grass are apple mousse,
　　Wild honey in the may.
Everything scrumptious, good and delicious
　　For you this fresh spring day.

VINCE CROSS

Stocking and Shirt

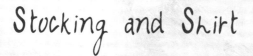

Stocking and shirt
　　Can trip and prance,
Though nobody's in them
　　To make them dance.
　　　See how they waltz
　　　　Or minuet,
　　　　　Watch the petticoat
　　　　　　Pirouette.
　　　　　　This is the dance
　　　　　　　Of stocking and shirt,
　　　　　　　When the wind puts on
　　　　　　　The white lace skirt.
　　　　　Old clothes and young clothes
　　　　Dance together,
　　　Twirling and whirling
　　In mad March weather.
　'Come!' cries the wind
　　To stocking and shirt.
　　　'Away!' cries the wind
　　　　To blouse and skirt.

Then clothes and wind
All pull together,
Tugging like mad
In the mad March weather.
Across the garden
They suddenly fly
And over the far hedge
High, high, high!
'Stop!' cries the housewife
But all too late,
Her clothes have passed
The furthest gate.
They are gone forever
In the bright blue sky,
And only the handkerchiefs
Wave good-bye.

JAMES REEVES

Child's Song in Spring

The silver birch is a dainty lady,
     She wears a satin gown;
The elm-tree makes the churchyard shady,
She will not live in town.

The English oak is a sturdy fellow;
He gets his green coat late;
The willow is smart in a suit of yellow,
While brown the beech trees wait.

Such a gay green gown God gives the larches –
As green as He is good!
The hazels hold up their arms for arches
When spring rides through the wood.

The chestnut's proud, and the lilac's pretty,
The poplar's gentle and tall,
But the plane tree's kind to the poor dull city –
I love him best of all!

E. NESBIT

Spring

Sunlight on the garden,
     Flowers on the hill,
The bathroom window open
And my elbows on the sill.

Blossom in the trees,
Buds and birds and leaves,
Sun so warm against my face
I've rolled up both my sleeves.

Singing from the kitchen,
A pale blue sky,
Daffodils among the grass
And washing out to dry.

MICHELLE MAGORIAN

25

The Spring Rabbit

Joyce Dunbar

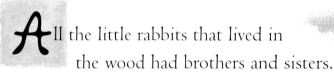

All the little rabbits that lived in
the wood had brothers and sisters.
All except Smudge.

'Why haven't I got a sister or brother?' he asked his mother.

'Wait until spring,' she answered.

Spring seemed a long way away.

Smudge watched on a cold autumn morning
as the other rabbits chased falling leaves. Then he had an idea. He
made a leaf rabbit with leafy broken twigs.

'You can be my brother,' he said to the leaf rabbit. 'Let's chase
each other down the hill.'

The leaf rabbit didn't answer.

Then the wind blew all the leaves away, leaving
only the bare twigs.

'Wait until spring,' said a mouse.

But spring was a long time
coming.

26

Later, the snow fell. Smudge made a snow rabbit.

'You can be my sister,' he said to the snow rabbit. 'Let's have a game of snowball.'

But the snow rabbit couldn't play snowball.

Next day, the snow rabbit melted.

'Wait until spring,' said a robin.

But spring was a long time coming.

When the snow melted, Smudge made a mud rabbit.

'You can be my brother,' he said to the mud rabbit. 'Let's splash about in the puddles.'

But the mud rabbit didn't splash about.

The rain came and washed it away.

'Wait until spring,' said a frog.

At last came the first signs of spring.

All the twigs were sprouting green shoots and the buds were beginning to show.

Smudge went looking for his brother. He looked in the hollows of the trees, but he found no sign of a brother, only a mouse hole, full of baby mice.

'There are no rabbits here,' said the mouse.

He looked in the bushes and brambles, but he didn't find a brother there either, only a bird's nest, with six speckled eggs.

'There are no rabbits here,' said the robin.

He looked in the reeds by the pond, but he didn't find a brother there either, only frogspawn full of tiny tadpoles.

'There are no rabbits here,' said the frog.

Smudge felt very sad and lonely. At last he went home.

'I can't find my spring brother anywhere,' he said to his mother.

'You were looking in all the wrong places,' she said, showing him three tiny bundles. 'See what we have here.'

Smudge was overjoyed. He had two baby brothers and a sister. As soon as they were hopping about he made them an enormous moss rabbit . . .

. . . and everyone knew that spring had come.

Spring

'My dear,' said Mrs Wren,
    'If Mrs Cuckoo comes to call,
I really think it would be best
To see her in the hall.
Explaining that our house
It is so very very small,
We have no room for paying guests
Or any guests at all.'

E. Lucia Turnbull

WREN

Little Brown Seed

Little brown seed, round and sound,
    Here I put you in the ground.

    You can sleep a week or two,
    Then — I'll tell you what to do:

You must grow some downward roots,
Then some tiny upward shoots.

    From those green shoots, folded sheaves
    Soon must come some healthy leaves.

    When the leaves have time to grow,
    Next a bunch of buds must show.

Last of all the buds must spread
Into blossoms white or red.

There, seed! I've done my best —
Please to grow and do the rest.

RODNEY BENNETT

30

Louder than Sparrows

Singing, singing,
    all the world is singing –
sparrows on the housetops,
    thrushes in the trees,
bees above the hawthorn
    crickets in the clover,
and, loudest of them all, sings
    JANE-SARAH LEAS,
louder than the sparrows,
    sweeter than the thrushes,
chirpier than the crickets,
    bolder than the bees,
listen! and you'll hear her,
    singing to the whole world,
singing with the springtime
    underneath the trees.

IVY O. EASTWICK

A Date with Spring

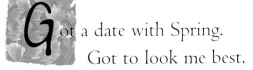

Got a date with Spring.
      Got to look me best.
Of all the trees
I'll be smartest dressed.

Perfumed breeze
behind me ear.
Pollen accessories
all in place.
Raindrop moisturizer
for me face.
Sunlight tints
to spruce up the hair.

What's the good of being a tree
if you can't flaunt your beauty?

Winter, I was naked.
Exposed as can be.
Me wardrobe took off
with the wind.
Life was a frosty slumber.
Now, Spring, here I come.
Can't wait to slip in
to me little green number.

JOHN AGARD

Cows

Half the time they munched the grass, and all the time
      they lay
Down in the water-meadows, the lazy month of May,
A-chewing,
A-mooing,
To pass the hours away.

   'Nice weather,' said the brown cow,
      'Ah,' said the white.
   'Grass is very tasty.'
      'Grass is all right.'

Half the time they munched the grass, and all the time
      they lay
Down in the water-meadows, the lazy month of May,
A-chewing
A-mooing,
To pass the hours away.

   'Rain coming,' said the brown cow,
      'Ah,' said the white.
   'Flies is very tiresome.'
      'Flies bite.'

Half the time they munched the grass, and all the time
     they lay
Down in the water-meadows, the lazy month of May,
A-chewing,
A-mooing,
To pass the hours away.

'Time to go,' said the brown cow,
    'Ah,' said the white.
'Nice chat. Very pleasant.'
    'Night.' 'Night.'

Half the time they munched the grass, and all the time
     they lay
Down in the water-meadows, the lazy month of May,
A-chewing,
A-mooing,
To pass the hours away.

JAMES REEVES

Carpet of Blue

It can happen, it can happen
Late in April, early May
You don't think you'll come across it
So it takes your breath away
You'll have entered on the hillside
Through the fence you always use
To the woods you always walk in
Round the way you always choose
When you stumble on the bluebells
And it seems a fact to you
That there's never been a carpet
Quite so beautiful or blue.

HIAWYN ORAM

Summer

Illustrated
by
Lydia Monks

ACKNOWLEDGEMENTS

The editor and publisher gratefully acknowledges permission to reproduce copyright material in this book:

'At the Seaside' by Tony Bradman from *Smile, Please!* published by Viking Kestrel 1987. Copyright © Tony Bradman, 1987. Reproduced by permission of Penguin Books Ltd.

'Seaweed' by Myra Cohn Livingston from *Wide Awake and Other Poems* by Myra Cohn Livingston. Copyright © Myra Cohn Livingston, 1959, 1987. Reproduced by permission of literary agent Marian Reiner.

'My Watering Can' by Stanley Cook from *The Poem Box* published by Blackie 1991. Copyright © The Estate of Stanley Cook. Reproduced by permission of Sarah Matthews, literary executor.

'The Seagull's Song' by June Crebbin from *Cows Moo, Cars Toot!* published by Viking Children's Books 1995. Copyright © June Crebbin, 1995. Reproduced by permission of Penguin Books Ltd.

'August Afternoon' by Marion Edey and Dorothy Grider from *Open the Door* published by Charles Scribner's Sons, NY, 1949. Reproduced by permission of Atheneum Books for Young Readers, an imprint of Simon & Schuster Children's Publishing Division.

'Summer Days' by Anne English from *Sit on the Roof and Holler* edited by Adrian Rumble, published by Bell & Hyman 1984. Copyright © Anne English, 1983. Reproduced by permission of the author.

'There are Big Waves' by Eleanor Farjeon from *Silver Sand and Snow* published by Michael Joseph. Reproduced by permission of David Higham Associates Ltd.

'Seaside' by Jean Kenward from *Poetry Corner 2* published by BBC Books 1993. Copyright © Jean Kenward, 1993. Reproduced by permission of the author.

'Donkey Doesn't Like It' by Thelma Lambert from *The Parent's Guide to Bedtime Stories* edited by Tony Bradman, published by Viking Kestrel 1989. Copyright © Thelma Lambert, 1989. Reproduced by permission of Penguin Books Ltd.

'Sand-between-the-Toes' by A. A. Milne from *When We Were Very Young* by A. A. Milne. Copyright under the Berne convention. Published by Methuen, an imprint of Egmont Children's Books Limited, London and used with permission.

'Summer Afternoon' by Cynthia Mitchell from *Poetry Corner Teachers' Notes* published by BBC Radio for Schools 1981. Copyright © Cynthia Mitchell, 1981. Reproduced by permission of the author.

'Come On into my Tropical Garden' by Grace Nichols from *Come On into my Tropical Garden* published by A & C Black Ltd 1988. Copyright © Grace Nichols, 1988. Reproduced by permission of Curtis Brown Ltd, London, on behalf of Grace Nichols.

'On the Beach' by Michael Rosen from *Tea in the Sugar Bowl, Potato in my Shoe* published by Walker Books Ltd. Copyright © Michael Rosen, 1986, 1987. Reproduced by permission of Walker Books Ltd., London.

'Song of Summer' by Margaret Wise Brown from *Nibble, Nibble* published by HarperCollins Publishers, USA. Text copyright © William R. Scott, Inc, 1959, renewed by Roberta Brown Rauch, 1987. Reproduced by permission of HarperCollins Publishers, USA.

Every effort has been made to trace copyright holders. The editor and publisher would like to hear from any copyright holders not acknowledged.

Song of Summer

Here comes a bunny
    The first to stray
Out of April
    And into May.

And here comes a robin
    The first to fly
Out of June
    And into July.

Here are the fireflies
    Last to remember
The end of August
    And first of September.

And here comes a caterpillar
    The last to creep
Out of summer
    And into sleep.

MARGARET WISE BROWN

39

At the Seaside

The day we went down to the seaside
    Was a day when we had such fun,
I paddled in the cold wet sea
And played in the warm summer sun.

I dug a big hole and buried
My dad very deep in the sand,
We covered up every bit of him —
Except for his head and his hands.

I had a lovely cold lolly,
I went for a donkey ride,
I found a sea shell and listened
To the whispering sea inside.

I built a great huge castle,
And my mum dug out a big moat,
Then we had a neat game of pirates,
And I sailed my little boat.

And when it was time to pack up,
To say goodbye to the sea,
I wasn't too sad because I had
My shell to take home with me.

Tony Bradman

41

Rosebud in June

It's a rosebud in June
          And the violets in bloom.
And small birds are singing
Love songs on each spray.
We'll pipe and we'll sing, love,
We'll dance in a ring, love,
Each lad with his lass,
All on the green grass.
And it's all to the plough
Where the oxen graze low,
And the lads and their lasses
Do sheep-shearing go.

TRADITIONAL

Summer Days

I'm looking for a hot spot.
A what spot?
A hot spot.
I'm looking for a hot spot
To lie out in the sun.
I'm looking for a hot spot
To play and have some fun.
I'm looking for a hot spot
To hit a ball and run.
Oh, I'm looking for a hot spot.
A what spot?
A hot spot.
I'm looking for a hot spot
Now summer has begun.

ANNE ENGLISH

43

August Afternoon

Where shall we go?
    What shall we play?
What shall we do
On a hot summer day?

We'll sit in the swing.
Go low. Go high.
And drink lemonade
Till the glass is dry.

One straw for you,
One straw for me,
In the cool green shade
Of the walnut tree.

MARION EDEY & DOROTHY GRIDER

There are Big Waves

There are big waves and little waves,
    Green waves and blue,
Waves you can jump over,
    Waves you dive thro',
Waves that rise up
    Like a great water wall,
Waves that swell softly
    And don't break at all,
Waves that can whisper,
    Waves that can roar,
    And tiny waves that run at you
        Running on the shore.

ELEANOR FARJEON

Little Pig and the Hot Dry Summer

MARGARET GORE

Are you sitting comfortably?
Then I'll begin.

'I wish it would rain!' said Little Pig.

There had been no rain for weeks and weeks, and all the pigs were puffing and grunting with the heat. In the field beyond the pigsties the ground was as hard as an overbaked cake.

No rain meant that there was no mud. And what Little Pig loved most of all was mud. Thick, squelchy, oozy *mud*! Little Pig would roll on his back, waving his four pink trotters in the air and squealing with delight.

'If *only* it would rain!' sighed Little Pig. 'This summer has been so hot and dry, and I *do* love a mucky roll in the mud!'

In the sty next door to Little Pig lived Big Pig. Big Pig was a terrible boaster.

'*I* could make it rain – if I *wanted* to, that is,' he said. None of the other pigs believed Big Pig. Especially Quick Pig, who had a sharp tongue.

Quick Pig said, 'Go on then, *make* it rain, Big Pig!'

'I — I don't think I have time just now,' replied Big Pig.

Slow Pig grunted, 'He knows he can't, that's why.'

Big Pig pretended to be busy rooting about for something to eat. Slow Pig had hardly moved all summer — except to eat. He just lay by the wall, snoring. Even Kind Pig, who was a most patient pig, grew tired of Slow Pig's snoring.

The weather grew hotter and hotter. And *still* no rain.

'I don't think I shall ever have a good, mucky roll in the mud again!' wept Little Pig.

'Of course you will, Little Pig,' said Kind Pig. 'I'm sure it must rain soon!'

And it *did* rain. That very night.

First came a few big spots. Splash, splash, splodge. Then it rained faster and faster, and heavier and heavier.

Now it was simply bucketing down! The rain hissed on the roof; it swept across the yard; it gushed down the drains.

It made a noise like a hundred pigs all drinking at once from a high trough!

But the trouble was, now that the rain had started it wouldn't stop.

47

It went on all the next day,
and all the next night, and
all the next day after that!

'It's never going to stop
raining!' squealed Little Pig.
Quick Pig blamed Big Pig.

'*You* made it rain —
and now you can't stop it!'

'It's not *my* fault,' grumbled
Big Pig.

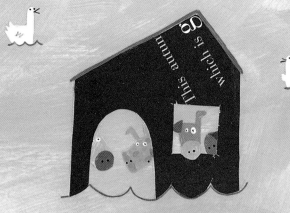

There was water everywhere. Even the
field became a lake. The ducks from the
pond were able to swim right up to the wall
of the pigsties. *Inside*, the pigs were huddled
together, squealing; and *outside* the ducks swam up
and down teasing them, and laughing their quacky laughs.

The water got higher and higher. Little Pig was frightened,
but Kind Pig said, 'Don't cry, Little Pig. Look, here is someone
coming to save us.'

It was Tom the farmhand. He came sailing across the field on a
wooden raft which he had just knocked together from an old door.

Tom put down a plank from the pigsties on to the raft, and
then the pigs walked across it. First Quick Pig — because he was
always first with everything (especially eating!).

Then Big Pig, because he had knocked everyone else out of the
way. Then Kind Pig, who showed Little Pig how to walk along the

plank without falling off, and lastly Slow Pig — it *had* to be
Slow Pig, didn't it!

The pigs sailed away on their raft, to a dry place on the other
side of the field. And there they had to stay, until, next morning,
they were awakened by Little Pig squealing and squealing.

'Wake up, wake up,' cried Little Pig. 'The sun's shining and all
the water has gone! We can go home.'

Little Pig was quite right. They did go home, but not by raft,
because there was no water left. They had to go by tractor, because
the whole field was a mass of — MUD.

'Squelchy, oozy, delicious MUD!' cried Little Pig. When they
reached home, the pigs trotted happily back into their own sties.
First Quick Pig, then Big Pig, then Kind Pig, and
last of all Slow Pig.

But where was *Little* Pig?

The pigs crowded to the wall and looked over
into the field.

There was Little Pig. He was lying on his back
in the mud, waving his four pink trotters in
the air and squealing with delight.

'I *do* love a good mucky roll!'
said Little Pig.

Come on into my Tropical Garden

Come on into my tropical garden
Come on in and have a laugh in
Taste my sugar cake and my pine drink
Come on in please come on in

And yes you can stand up in my hammock
and breeze out in my trees
you can pick my hibiscus
and kiss my chimpanzees

O you can roll up in the grass
and if you pick up a flea
I'll take you down for a quick-dip wash
    in the sea
believe me there's nothing better
for getting rid of a flea
than having a quick-dip wash in the sea

Come on into my tropical garden
Come on in please come on in

GRACE NICHOLS

50

Summer Afternoon

Bumble bee so busy
    Round the hollyhocks,
Working all the summer
    In your furry socks,
Don't you wish that you could
    Have a holiday?
Busy, buzzy, Bumble,
    Don't you ever play?

CYNTHIA MITCHELL

My Watering Can

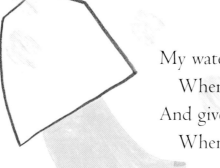

When it's hot I work in the garden
    With my plastic watering can
That's the same shiny red
    As a Post Office van.

My watering can brings rain
    When there isn't a cloud in the sky
And gives the flowers a shower
    When they are dusty and dry.

I water the grass on the lawn
    That the sun has toasted brown;
I water the steps to the lawn
    And watch the drops drip down.

I water the path again and again
And make a winding stream;
I sprinkle my motor car
Until it's perfectly clean.

I water an upturned bucket
And empty flowerpot
And anything that needs to be cooled
When the sun has made it hot.

STANLEY COOK

On the Beach

There's a man over there
  and he's sitting in the sand.
He buried himself at tea-time,
now he's looking for his hand.

  There's a boy over there
  and he's sitting on the rocks
  eating apple crumble,
  washing dirty socks.

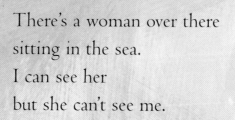

  There's a woman over there
  sitting in the sea.
  I can see her
  but she can't see me.

  There's a girl over there
  and she's sitting on a chair.
  Standing just behind her
  is a big grizzly bear.

  MICHAEL ROSEN

Seaweed

Seaweed from high tide
where sand and breakers meet
gummy
on my tummy,
slippery
on my feet.

MYRA COHN LIVINGSTON

Donkey Doesn't Like It

Thelma Lambert

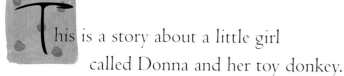

T his is a story about a little girl
called Donna and her toy donkey.
   Donkey was grey and cuddly with long floppy ears and Donna
loved him. Donkey went everywhere with her. And at night he
slept nestled up to Donna in her bed. The little girl would pretend
that Donkey could talk.

'Donkey doesn't like it!' she would
say if they had spinach for dinner.
   'Donkey doesn't want to!' she
would say when told to go to bed.
   Now, one day Mum had to go into
hospital. And it was decided that Dad
would take Donna to stay with Granny
and Grandpa.
   'Donkey doesn't want to go to
Grandpa's!' said Donna grumpily.

'But they have a little house for the summer, right by the sea!' said Dad. 'You'll love it there.'

Donna had never ever been to the seaside in her life. She asked Mum what it was like, the sea.

'Lovely!' said Mum with a smile. 'Lots and lots of water. Sometimes it's blue and sometimes it's green . . . and there are children paddling, people sailing, fish swimming . . .'

The next morning dawned bright and sunny and Dad started the car. The little girl and her toy donkey sat in the back looking glum.

It was a very long journey and Donna was soon fast asleep. When she woke, she saw out of the window lots and lots of green water. And there were children paddling. Donna thought this must be the seaside!

'No!' laughed Dad. 'It's only a big pond!'

They drove on. Donna fell asleep a second time. And when she woke, she saw out of the window lots and lots of *blue* water, and people sailing boats. This *must* be the sea, thought Donna.

But Dad said no, it was just a lake. Donna slept once more, and this time she woke up because Dad had stopped the car.

'We're there!' cried Dad.

Stiffly Donna climbed out of the car and
rubbed her eyes. But she couldn't see any water at all.
Just sand as far as the eye could see.

'Where is it?' she said. 'I can't see any sea!'

Dad pointed. Sparkling in the sun, far, far away, was a thin silver
line. *That* was the sea! The tide had gone so far out there was only
an enormous beach left.

'Donkey doesn't like it,' said Donna. 'It's too big.
Too much sand!'

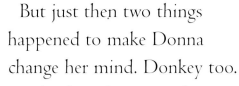

But just then two things
happened to make Donna
change her mind. Donkey too.

The first thing was that
Donna saw — walking slowly
across the sand — Granny and
Grandpa! They were wearing
their straw sun-hats. Grandpa
was bringing ice creams for
everyone!

The other thing that happened was that from the opposite direction came – walking slowly across the sand – two donkeys! They had grey hair, just like Granny and Grandpa, and they wore straw sun-hats too. But their hats had little holes for their ears to poke through!

'LOOK, Donkey! Here are YOUR Granny and Grandpa!' exclaimed Donna. 'You've come to visit THEM!'

That night in the cosy little house by the sea, Donna and Donkey snuggled down in a warm bed. Granny came in to kiss them goodnight.

'I was thinking,' said Granny. 'Would Donkey like me to make him a little sun-hat, like the real donkeys have on the beach?'

Donna said he definitely *would*.

'Granny! I think I'm going to like it here!' said Donna, tucking the blanket round her toy donkey. 'And Donkey says he likes it too!'

Sunflakes

If sunlight fell like snowflakes,
     gleaming yellow and so bright,
we could build a sunman,
we could have a sunball fight,
we could watch the sunflakes
drifting in the sky.
We could go sleighing
in the middle of July
through sundrifts and sunbanks,
we could ride a sunmobile,
and we could touch sunflakes —
I wonder how they'd feel.

FRANK ASCH

Sand-between-the-toes

I went down to the shouting sea,
    Taking Christopher down with me,
For Nurse had given us sixpence each —
And down we went to the beach.

   We had sand in the eyes and the ears and the nose,
   And sand in the hair, and sand-between-the-toes,
   Whenever a good nor'-wester blows,
      Christopher is certain of
      Sand-between-the-toes.

The sea was galloping grey and white;
Christopher clutched his sixpence tight;
We clambered over the humping sand —
And Christopher held my hand.

   We had sand in the eyes and the ears and the nose,
   And sand in the hair, and sand-between-the-toes.
   Whenever a good nor'-wester blows,
      Christopher is certain of
      Sand-between-the-toes.

                    A. A. MILNE

The Seagull's Song

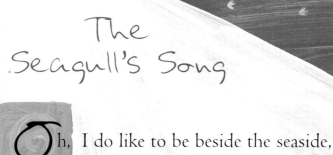

Oh, I do like to be beside the seaside,
　　I do like to be beside the sea,
I do like to soar above a seaside town,
See the boats in the harbour bobbing up and down.

Oh, I do like to be beside the seaside,
There is nowhere that I would rather be,
I can perch on sailing ships,
Grab a meal of fish and chips,
Beside the seaside, beside the sea.

JUNE CREBBIN

Seaside

C ome – o do come
quickly
down to the beach
with me
before a foot
has broken it!
Green, green
the sea,
but the sand
is golden
listening
to the tide
with wet weed
and white shells
and bits of wood beside . . .

The waves are small
and distant,
but look, they're coming
near,
and soon they'll reach
the castle
and the moat we've scrabbled
here.
Dig, dig
your fastest!
Build, build
a wall –
after the water's
touched it, there'll be
nothing left at all.

JEAN KENWARD

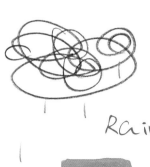

Rain in Summer

How beautiful is the rain!
    After the dust and heat,
In the broad and fiery street,
In the narrow lane,
How beautiful is the rain!

How it clatters along the roofs,
Like the tramp of hoofs!
How it gushes and struggles out
From the throat of the overflowing spout!
Across the window pane
It pours and pours;
And swift and wide,
With a muddy tide,
Like a river down the gutter roars
The rain, the welcome rain!

HENRY WADSWORTH LONGFELLOW

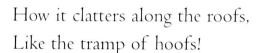

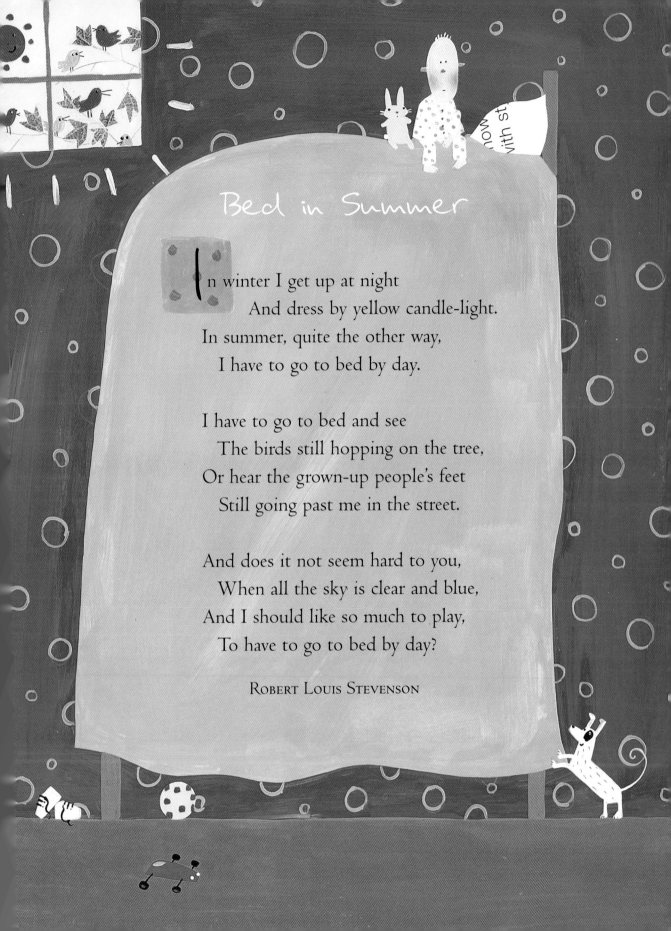

Bed in Summer

In winter I get up at night
    And dress by yellow candle-light.
In summer, quite the other way,
    I have to go to bed by day.

I have to go to bed and see
    The birds still hopping on the tree,
Or hear the grown-up people's feet
    Still going past me in the street.

And does it not seem hard to you,
    When all the sky is clear and blue,
And I should like so much to play,
    To have to go to bed by day?

ROBERT LOUIS STEVENSON

Swallow

Fly away, fly away over the sea,
    Sun-loving swallow, for summer is done;
Come again, come again, come back to me,
Bringing the summer and bringing the sun.

CHRISTINA ROSSETTI

Autumn

Illustrated by
RUTH RIVERS

ACKNOWLEDGEMENTS

The editor and publisher gratefully acknowledges permission to reproduce the following copyright material:

'I'm a Tree' by Tony Bradman from *Smile, Please!* published by Viking Kestrel 1987. Copyright © Tony Bradman, 1987. Reproduced by permission of Penguin Books Ltd.

'Conker Collectors' and 'Goodnight' by June Crebbin from *Cows Moo, Cars Toot!* published by Viking Children's Books 1995. Copyright © June Crebbin, 1995. Reproduced by permission of Penguin Books Ltd.

'Johnny Appleseed' from *Stories for Five-Year-Olds* by Stephen and Sara Corrin published by Faber & Faber Ltd. Reproduced by permission of Faber & Faber Ltd.

'Horse Chestnuts' by John Cotton from *The Crystal Zoo* published by Oxford University Press 1985. Copyright © John Cotton, 1985. Reproduced by permission of the author.

'Something Told the Wild Geese' by Rachel Field from *Poems* by Rachel Field. Copyright 1934 Macmillan Publishing Company; copyright renewed © 1962 Arthur S. Pederson. Reproduced by permission of Simon & Schuster books for Young Readers, an imprint of Simon & Schuster Children's Publishing Division

'About Caterpillars' by Aileen Fisher from *In the Woods, In the Meadow* by Aileen Fisher. Copyright © Aileen Fisher, 1965, 1993. Reproduced by permission of Literary agent Marian Reiner.

'September Is' by Bobbi Katz. Copyright © Bobbi Katz, 1992. Reproduced by permission of the author.

'The Kite' by Jean Kenward from *Seasons, A Poetry Collection* published by Blackie 1989. Copyright © Jean Kenward, 1989. Reproduced by permission of Penguin Books Ltd.

'Autumn Leaves' by Eve Merriam from *Jamboree, Rhymes for All Times* by Eve Merriam. Copyright © Eve Merriam, 1962, 1964, 1966, 1973, 1984. Reproduced by permission of literary agent Marian Reiner.

'The Hedgehog' by Ian Serraillier from *Happily Ever After* published by Oxford University Press 1963. Reproduced by permission of Anne Serraillier.

'Acorn' by Jill Townsend from *Seed Poems* by John Foster, published by Oxford University Press 1990. Copyright © Jill Townsend, 1990. Reproduced by permission of the author.

'The Prize Pumpkin' by Colin West from *Puffin Annual No.2* published by Penguin Books 1975. Copyright © Colin West, 1975. Reproduced by permission of the author.

'Harvest Festival' by Irene Yates from *Seed Poems* by John Foster, published by Oxford University Press 1990. Copyright © Irene Yates. Reproduced by permission of the author.

Every effort has been made to trace copyright holders. The editor and publisher would like to hear from any copyright holders not acknowledged.

Goodbye to Summer

Summer is gone with all its roses,
    Its sun and perfume and sweet flowers,
Its warm air and refreshing showers:
And even Autumn closes.

    Yea, Autumn's chilly self is going
    And Winter comes which is much colder;
    Each day the hoar-frost waxes bolder,
    And the last buds cease blowing.

    CHRISTINA ROSSETTI

The Hedgehog

There's a hedgehog in the garden – come and see.
When he's still, he's like a pincushion that breathes.
When he moves, he's like a fat freckled mouse, following me
All over the place with pitter-patter feet.
He snorts and snuffs and sniffs my shoe,
Then hauls himself over the rise.

We'll introduce him to the cat. But she runs away
Into the box tree, all hidden save her eyes
And nose and twitching tail –
Then suddenly leaps out and pounces.
(Can you blame her? He's drunk all
Her saucerful of milk, three fluid ounces.)

Caught?
  Not likely. She pulls up short
    And dances and prances and saws
The air all round him, mighty dainty with her paws;
    Then, defeated, slinks away
    To sulk or chase less prickly prey.

  It's chilly now and getting late.
We'll cover him with a pile of autumn leaves
    And let him hide or even hibernate.
  In the morning we'll creep
Over the lawn and part the leaves and peer
    Inside, and see if he's lying there asleep.
      I hope he is . . .

IAN SERRAILLIER

I'm a Tree

Autumn leaves,
In the breeze
Falling down
On the ground.

On my knees
In the leaves,
Rolling round
On the ground.

Look at me –
I'm a tree,
Leaves all brown
And falling down!

TONY BRADMAN

Harvest Festival

Cabbages, cauliflowers,
    crisp, crunchy swedes,
peppers and parsnips
and melons with seeds;
Onions and mushrooms,
potatoes for chips,
tomatoes, bananas
and apples with pips;
Stick beans and broad beans
and beans in a tin,
blackcurrants so juicy
they run down your chin;
Cornflakes for breakfast
and mangoes for tea —
Come to our harvest
and give thanks with me.

IRENE YATES

Conker Collectors

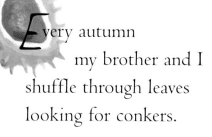

Every autumn
my brother and I
shuffle through leaves
looking for conkers.

He bakes his in the oven,
soaks them in vinegar,
threads them on a string
and bashes them.

But I pile mine up
on the windowsill
and just look.

JUNE CREBBIN

The Leaves in a Frolic

The leaves had a wonderful frolic,
      They danced to the wind's loud song,
They whirled, and they floated, and scampered,
They circled and flew along.

The moon saw the little leaves dancing,
Each looked like a small brown bird.
The man in the moon smiled and listened,
And this is the song he heard.

The North Wind is calling, is calling,
And we must whirl round and round,
And when our dancing is ended
We'll make a warm quilt for the ground.

ANONYMOUS

Home is Best

RICHARD WILSON

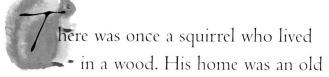

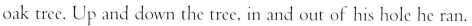

There was once a squirrel who lived
in a wood. His home was an old
oak tree. Up and down the tree, in and out of his hole he ran.

When summer was over, he made a cosy nest in the hole, and put all kinds of nuts in it so that he'd have plenty to eat in the winter, when there were no nuts to be found.

While he worked away at his winter store and home, he heard the birds chirping away to each other. They were all talking about the long journey they were going to make.

'Where are you going?' asked the squirrel.

'To a far-away land where there is no winter,' said one.

'Where the trees do not lose their leaves!'

'Where there are plenty of
flowers and nuts!'

'Where the sun shines
warmly all day long,'
said the rest.

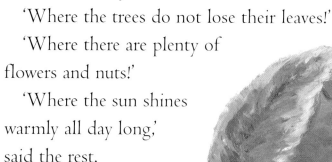

'It sounds wonderful,' said the squirrel. 'Could I go too?'

'Why not – just follow us over the blue hills.'

'When will you go?'

'Any day now,' said the birds. 'The swallows will go first, then the linnets will go, then the geese will go, and you can't miss them.'

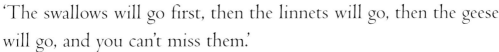

'I'll think it over,' said the squirrel, and went on building his nest. But when a cold east wind came, and the leaves began to fall, the squirrel thought of the warm land where the sun shone warmly all day long, where there were plenty of flowers and nuts, where the trees did not lose their leaves, and where there was no winter.

One day the squirrel made up his mind to follow the birds. On and on he went all day, but the blue hills still seemed as far away as ever, and the birds were soon out of sight.

'If only I had wings,' said he as he stopped to rest.

Just then a big hawk flew down and picked up the squirrel.

It was going to carry him away and eat him, when another hawk had the same idea, and tried to snatch him from the first.

They began to fight
over the squirrel, and in
the fight, the first dropped
him. Down, down he fell,
right on to the top of a
big oak tree.

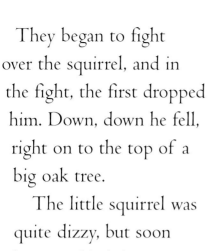

The little squirrel was
quite dizzy, but soon
he scrambled down
the tree, out of
sight of the
birds.

And what do you
think? In their fight, the hawks
had flown back to the squirrel's
wood and this was his very own oak tree.
He soon found his hole, and he crawled
into his warm nest and ate some nuts.
Then he curled up and went to sleep.
After that he always stayed
at home for the winter.

September Is

September is
    when yellow pencils
in brand new eraser hats
      bravely wait on perfect points —
ready to march across miles of lines
        in empty notebooks —
      and
September is
    when a piece of chalk
skates across the board —
    swirling and looping —
until it spells your new teacher's
    name.

Bobbi Katz

Seeds

Seeds that twist and seeds that twirl
  Seeds with wings which spin and whirl;

Seeds that float on thistledown
  Seeds in coats of glossy brown;

Seeds that burst with popping sounds
  From their pods to reach the ground;

Seeds with hooks that clutch and cling
  Seeds I plant for flowers next spring.

HILDA I. ROSTRON

Happy Apple

If I were an apple and grew on a tree,
    I think I'd fall down on a nice boy like me;
I wouldn't stay there giving nobody joy,
I'd fall down at once and say: 'Eat me, my boy.'

ANONYMOUS

Acorn

Sitting in its fat little egg-cup,
    Humpty Dumpty among the leaves
in its knobbly green trousers,
holding its tummy like a secret,
the secret of a new oak tree.

JILL TOWNSEND

Down
  down
    down
      Red
        yellow
          brown
Autumn leaves tumble down,
  Autumn leaves crumble down,
    Autumn leaves bumble down,
      Flaking and shaking,
        Tumbledown leaves.

Autumn
Leaves

            Skittery
             Flittery
            Rustle by
            Hustle by
      Crackle and crunch
      In a snappety bunch.

Run and catch
Run and snatch
Butterfly leaves
Sailboat leaves
Windstorm leaves.
Can you catch them?

Swoop,
Scoop,
Pile them up
In a stompy pile and
Jump
Jump
JUMP!

Eve Merriam

The Prize Pumpkin

They seized it, they squeezed it,
They gave it funny looks,
They teased it, they eased it,
They looked it up in books.
They tethered it, they weathered it,
They even tarred and feathered it,
And when they could, they measured it
(It came to seven foot).

They gave it a prod, they gave it a poke,
They sang it a song, they told it a joke.

They ran to it, they walked to it,
They then began to talk to it,
They lathered it (they rathered it
Was clean as it could be),
They smothered it, they mothered it,
They fathered and they brothered it,
They watered it, they daughtered it,
And sat it on their knee.

They gave it a slap, they gave it a punch,
They cut it in bits and had it for lunch!

COLIN WEST

84

Autumn Fires

*I*n the other gardens
    And all up the vale,
From the autumn bonfires
    See the smoke trail!

Pleasant summer over
And all the summer flowers,
    The red fire blazes,
The grey smoke towers.

Sing a song of seasons!
    Something bright in all!
Flowers in the summer,
    Fires in the fall!

ROBERT LOUIS
STEVENSON

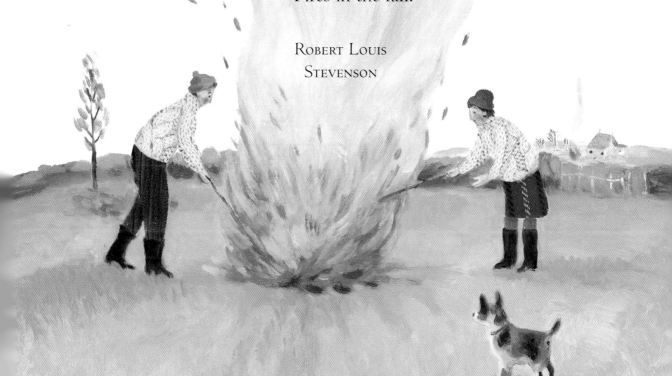

Johnny Appleseed

Traditional,
retold by
Stephen Corrin

any years ago, when your grandfather's
great-grandfather was still a child,
there lived a boy in Boston in America called
John Chapman. He loved the countryside,
the flowers and trees and woods, and he knew all
about the beasts and birds who lived in them.
His favourite tree was the apple-tree. He loved climbing apple-trees
and munching an apple as he rested on their branches.

Once as he was happily chewing a juicy apple he picked out a
few of the little brown apple-pips and gazed at them thoughtfully.

'If I planted these seeds,' he said aloud, 'the whole countryside
would be filled with apple-trees.' So when he grew to be a man,
John Chapman started roaming the country with a large sack full
of apple-seeds on his back and a cooking pan slung round his
shoulder. He would stop every now and then and plant a seed or

give a handful to a passer-by. He was so happy and friendly that he became known to everyone for miles around. People would give him food and shelter in return for his apple-pips and they called him Johnny Appleseed.

Soon he roamed farther and farther away from his home town, planting apple-seeds wherever he went. He planted his seeds up and down the country, in the bare brown earth in the autumn.

After the winter the spring came and Johnny Appleseed would go back to each place to see the little green shoots pushing up through the earth.

Everywhere baby apple-trees sprang up and grew. In time they would blossom and bear fruit, and his eye twinkled with happiness when he thought of all the children who would one day enjoy all those wonderful apples – the Pippins and the Russets and the Pound Sweets as well as the baked apples and apple-jellies and toffee-apples they would provide.

On his wanderings Johnny Appleseed always slept in the open air and cooked his own meals. He met many wolves, foxes, deer and even bears and made friends with them all. Even when it snowed he slept out in the open and showed no fear. Rather than send away a bear and her cub from the hollow log where they were sheltering, he preferred to remain in the cold.

But one day in the bitter winter when snow covered all the beloved apple-trees which he had planted, he caught a chill and was very ill. A mother bear and her cub watched him sadly as he lay, and then wandered off. Luckily some Indians saw the bears and followed their trail till it led them to where Johnny Appleseed lay. They at once recognized him as their old friend who had planted the wonderful seeds in their land. They took him to their tepee and gave him their medicines and they gave him good food and they looked after him with tender care.

Then one sunny morning Johnny Appleseed opened his eyes and smiled at his faithful Indian friends. He knew they had saved his life. He wandered out into the fields. The snow had melted from the apple-trees and in the early spring their fragrant blossoms gleamed in the sun.

Johnny was now determined to wander even farther but he always returned to visit old friends and especially the Indians who had saved his life. On and on he went, tramping hundreds of miles along riversides, up hill and down dale, planting the brown pips wherever he went.

The years rolled by and Johnny Appleseed was now an old man with long white hair and flowing beard. But his cheeks were rosy from the fresh air and wind and his black eyes always twinkled with joy and kindness.

Children would gather round to hear the stories of his wanderings and wherever he went the settlers in this new land knew him as the man who made their countryside rich with beautiful trees where once there was nothing but the bare brown earth.

Horse Chestnuts

Autumn's special toys,
　　There is something about the newness of them,
Their gloss, the colour of burnished horses,
Their richness protected from their fall
By those thick green cases,
So that we can harvest them
Safe in their nests
Of last year's debris of leaves,
To pocket them
For treasure or for play.
Though they will never be
Quite so beautiful again,
As that first moment
When we saw them peep pristine
From their soft-spiked shells.

JOHN COTTON

About Caterpillars

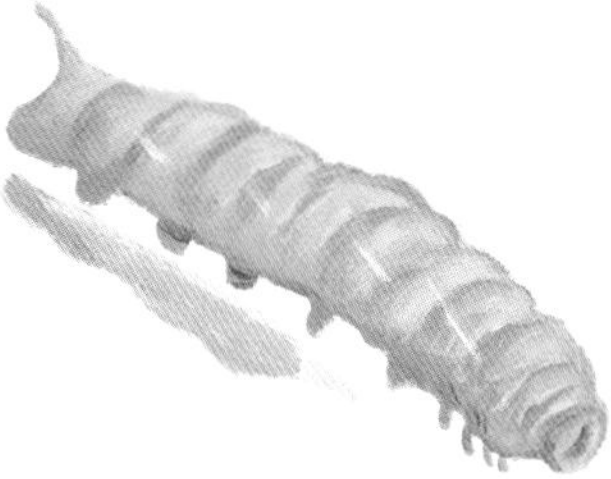

What about caterpillars?
Where do they crawl
when the stars say, 'Frost',
and the leaves say, 'Fall'?

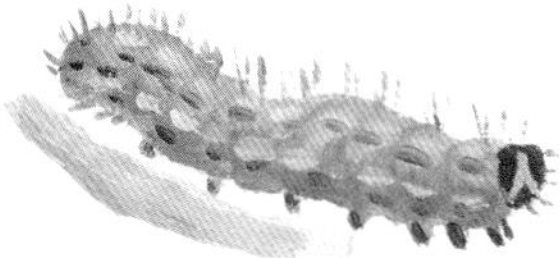

Some go to sleep
in a white silk case
when the winds say, 'Blow!'
and the clouds say, 'Race!'

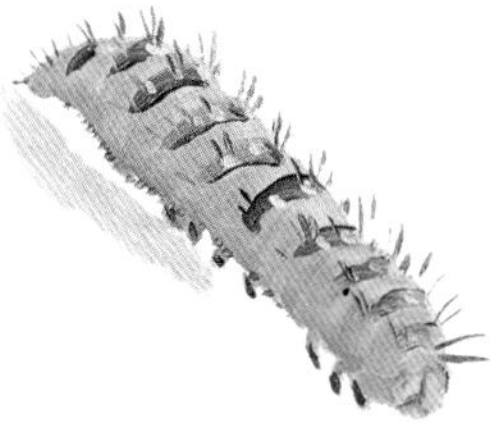

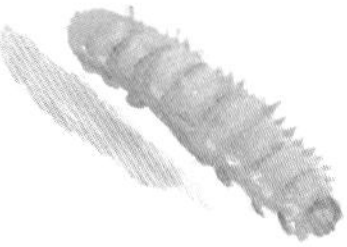

Some sleep in bags
of woven brown
or curl in a ball
when the year says, 'Frown'.

None has the least
little urge to know
what the world is like
when the sky says, 'Snow'.

AILEEN FISHER

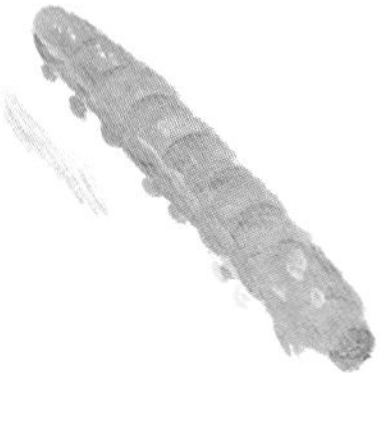

The Kite

Up on the top
    of Birdlip Hill
I saw a person
 standing still;
  I saw a person
  with a string,
   and at the end of it
   a thing
   that dived and soared
   and leaped and fell . . .
and rose again . . .

I could not tell
whether it were
a bird in flight —
it was so airy
and so light —
and yet he held it
on a string.

It tugged and tugged
like anything,
and still he would not
let it go
but hung onto
the coil below,
and up it climbed
and down, and then
in lilting spirals
up again.
He laughed to watch it
plunge and play.

I nearly saw him
blow away.

JEAN KENWARD

October's Party

October gave a party;
  The leaves in hundreds came –
The Chestnuts, Oaks and Maples,
  The leaves of every name.

The sunshine spread a carpet,
  And everything was grand,
Miss Weather led the dancing,
  Professor Wind the band.

The Chestnuts came in yellow,
  The Oaks in crimson dressed;
The lovely Missus Maple
  In scarlet looked her best.

All balanced to their partners,
  And gaily fluttered by,
The sight was like a rainbow
  New fallen from the sky.

GEORGE COOPER

Something Told the Wild Geese

Something told the wild geese
 It was time to go,
Though the fields lay golden
 Something whispered 'Snow!'
Leaves were green and stirring,
 Berries lustre-glossed,
But beneath warm feathers
 Something cautioned 'Frost!'

All the sagging orchards
 Steamed with amber spice,
But each wild beast stiffened
 At remembered ice.
Something told the wild geese
 It was time to fly —
Summer sun was on their wings,
 Winter in their cry.

RACHEL FIELD

Goodnight

'Goodnight,' said the frog, 'I am
    burrowing deep
Into the mud for my winter sleep.'

'Goodnight,' said the hedgehog, 'I'm off to
    my nest,
It's time I went for a good long rest.'

'Goodnight,' said the bat, 'my feet are
    strong,
I'll hang in a cave the winter long.'

'Goodnight,' said the dormouse, 'I shall be
Curled in my nest at the foot of the tree.'

JUNE CREBBIN

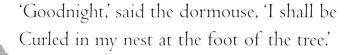

Winter

Illustrated by
Tom Saeker

ACKNOWLEDGEMENTS

The editor and publisher gratefully acknowledges permission to reproduce the following copyright material:

'Mrs Bear' by Finola Akister from *Before You Go To Bed* by Finola Akister published by Viking Kestrel 1989.
Copyright © Finola Akister, 1989. Reproduced by permission of Penguin Books Ltd.

'Brown Bear's Wedding' by Martine Beck, published by L'ecole es Loisirs 1989. Text copyright © Martine Beck, 1989.
Reproduced by permission of David Grossman Literary Agency Ltd.

'Paws' by Stanley Cook from *A Very First Poetry Book* edited by John Foster published by Oxford University Press 1984.
Copyright © The Estate of Stanley Cook. Reproduced by permission of Sarah Matthews, literary executor.

'No School Today' and 'Winter Trees' by June Crebbin from *Cows Moo, Cars Toot!* published by Viking Children's Books 1995.
Copyright © June Crebbin, 1995. Reproduced by permission of Penguin Books Ltd.

'Snow' by Walter de la Mare from *The Complete Poems of Walter de la Mare* published 1969. Reproduced by permission of The Literary
Trustees of Walter de la Mare, and the Society of Authors as their representative.

'Winter Excursions' by Gavin Ewart from *Like It or Not* published by The Bodley Head 1992.
Copyright © Gavin Ewart 1992. Reproduced by permission of The Random House Group Ltd.

'The Harbour Wall' by Wes Magee from *Seaside Poems* published by Oxford University Press, 1998.
Copyright © Wes Magee, 1998. Reproduced by permission of Oxford University Press.

'Joe' by David McCord from *One at a Time* published by Little, Brown and Company Inc.
Copyright © David McCord, 1952. Reproduced by permission of Little, Brown and Company Inc.

'The Snowman' by Roger McGough from *Sky in the Pie* published by Viking Children's Books 1983. Copyright © Roger McGough,
1983. Reproduced by permission of The Peters, Fraser & Dunlop Group Ltd on behalf of Roger McGough.

'First Snow in the Street' by Brian Patten from *The Utter Nutters* published by Viking Children's Books 1994.
Copyright © Brian Patten, 1994. Reproduced by permission of Rogers, Coleridge & White Ltd on behalf of the author.

'It's Winter, It's Winter' by Kit Wright from *Hot Dog and Other Poems* published by Kestrel 1981.
Copyright © Kit Wright, 1981. Reproduced by permission of Penguin Books Ltd.

'February Twilight' by Sara Teasdale from *The Collected Poems of Sara Teasdale*. Copyright ©   1926 by Macmillan Publishing Company,
renewed 1954 by Mamie T. Wheless. Reproduced by permission of Scribner, a Division of Simon & Schuster.

Every effort has been made to trace copyright holders. The editor and publisher would like to hear from any
copyright holders not acknowledged.

Mrs Bear

Mrs Bear had hibernated
All the winter through.
She went to bed and slept a lot,
There was nothing else to do.
The ground was cold and frozen hard,
The winds were fierce and chill,
So she and little Baby Bear
Slept on and on, until
One morning Mrs Bear woke up
And she said to herself, said she,
'I think the sun is shining,
I'll just pop out and see.'
So Baby Bear and Mrs Bear
Got up and left their den,
Outside the snow was falling fast
So they went back in again.
'I fear, my dear,' said Mrs Bear,
'It's really very plain,
We have woken up too early.'
So they went to sleep again.

FINOLA AKISTER

November

The leaves are fading and falling,
   The winds are rough and wild,
The birds have ceased their calling,
   But let me tell you, my child,

Though day by day, as it closes,
Doth darker and colder grow,
The roots of the bright red roses
Will keep alive in the snow.

And when the Winter is over,
The boughs will get new leaves,
The quail come back to the clover,
And the swallow back to the eaves.

The robin will wear on his bosom
A vest that is bright and new,
And the loveliest way-side blossom
Will shine with the sun and dew.

The leaves today are whirling,
The brooks are dry and dumb,
But let me tell you, my darling,
The Spring will be sure to come.

There must be rough, cold weather,
And winds and rains so wild;
Not all good things together
Come to us here, my child.

So, when some dear joy loses
Its beauteous summer glow,
Think how the roots of the roses
Are kept alive in the snow.

ALICE CARY

Summer fading, winter comes —
    Frosty mornings, tingling thumbs,
Window robins, winter rooks,
    And the picture story-books.

Water now is turned to stone
    Nurse and I can walk upon;
Still we find the flowing brooks
    In the picture story-books.

All the pretty things put by,
    Wait upon the children's eye,
Sheep and shepherds, trees and crooks,
    In the picture story-books.

We may see how all things are,
    Seas and cities, near and far,
And the flying fairies' looks,
    In the picture story-books.

How am I to sing your praise,
    Happy chimney-corner days,
Sitting safe in nursery nooks,
    Reading picture story-books?

ROBERT LOUIS STEVENSON

Picture
Books
in
Winter

The Harbour Wall

In winter
    when the wind blows wild
and the sea's as grey
    as a muddy puddle,

the harbour wall
    curls its long arm
around the boats
    bobbing in a huddle.

'I'll keep you safe,'
the wall seems to say.
'Come here.' And it gives
    the boats a cuddle.

WES MAGEE

Snow

No breath of wind,
      No gleam of sun —
Still the white snow
Whirls softly down —
Twig and bough
And blade and thorn
All in an icy
Quiet, forlorn.
Whispering, rustling,
Through the air,
On sill and stone,
Roof — everywhere,

It heaps its powdery
Crystal flakes,
Of every tree
A mountain makes;
Till pale and faint
At shut of day
Stoops from the West
One wintry ray.
And, feathered in fire,
Where ghosts the moon,
A robin shrills
His lonely tune.

WALTER DE LA MARE

104

No School Today

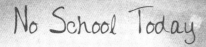

N o school today,
    Closed by snow,
We heard it on the radio.

' 's no good,'
  We said to each other,
  'We'll just have to go
    Sledging and sliding
    Bravely hiding
      Our keen disappointment . . .'

        'Yabba-dabba-doo!'

JUNE CREBBIN

Ridiculous!

MICHAEL COLEMAN

'Ho-hum,' yawned Mr Tortoise.
    'Winter is here.'
  'So it is,' yawned Mrs Tortoise.
'Come on, Shelley, time for bed.'
   'But I don't feel sleepy yet,' said Shelley.
   Ridiculous! cried Mr Tortoise.
'All tortoises go to sleep for the winter.'
    'Why?' asked Shelley.
    'Because it's cold outside and there's no food.'
    'But I don't want to go to sleep,' said Shelley.
'I want to see what winter is like!'
    Ridiculous! cried Mr and Mrs Tortoise together.
'Whoever heard of a tortoise out in winter?'
    Soon Mr Tortoise began to snore . . . and not long after
that Mrs Tortoise began to snore . . . and not
long after *that*, Shelley left her warm bed
of leaves and out she went through a
hole in the shed to see what
winter was like.

Outside the shed, Shelley blinked. There was
snow and ice everywhere, even on the duck pond and the hill.
As she lumbered along, a duck spotted her.

'A tortoise out in winter?' quacked the duck. *'Ridiculous!'*

'No it isn't,' said Shelley.

'Oh no? Then let me see you break through the
ice to get food like *I* can. Ha-quack-ha!'

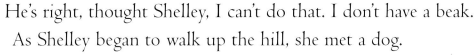

He's right, thought Shelley, I can't do that. I don't have a beak.
As Shelley began to walk up the hill, she met a dog.

'A tortoise out in winter?' barked the dog. *'Ridiculous!'*

'No it isn't,' said Shelley, feeling a bit cross.

'Oh no? Then let me see you keep warm by
running around like *I* can. Ha-woof-ha!'

He's right, thought Shelley sadly.
I can't do that, either.

The dog ran off after a cat, but the cat jumped on to the branch of a tree. She looked down at Shelley.

'A tortoise out in winter?' miaowed the cat. *'Ridiculous!'*

'No it isn't,' said Shelley, even more crossly.

'Oh no? Then let me see you run into a nice warm house as quickly as *I* can. Ha-miaow-ha!'

She's right, thought Shelley, shivering with cold. I can't run like a dog or a cat. I'm much too slow!

The cat raced off into her house before the dog could catch her, and Shelley trudged on up to the top of the hill, where she met a bird.

'A tortoise out in winter?' cheeped the bird. *'Ridiculous!'*

'No it isn't,' snapped Shelley.

'Oh no? Then let me see you fly off home to cuddle up with your family like *I* can. Ha-cheep-ha!'

Of course I can't fly, thought Shelley. I can't even hop!

Shelley felt cold and miserable. She remembered her lovely warm bed and a tear trickled down her cheek. They're *all* right, she thought. A tortoise out in winter *is* ridiculous!

Sadly she crept behind a shed where nobody would see her crying . . .

and slipped on a big patch of ice! Shelley fell
over backwards, and began to slide down the hill.
Faster and faster she went… faster than a *dog*
could run… faster than a *cat* … until
suddenly she hit a bump… and flew into
the air like a *bird*.

Wheeee!

Down she came again, and
landed on the icy duck pond.
She slithered towards her hole in
the shed … but it was all covered
up with ice!

'Ha-quack-ha, what did I say?
Where's your beak to break the ice with?'

The duck fell about laughing.

'No, I don't have a beak,' thought Shelley. 'But I *do* have… *a shell!*'

And tucking her head inside it, Shelley smashed her way through
the ice, into the shed and home!

Mrs Tortoise woke up as she heard all the noise.

'You haven't been outside, have you, Shelley?' she asked.

'Outside?' said Shelley, snuggling into bed.

'Whoever heard of a tortoise out in winter?'

And before you could say *'Ridiculous!'*

Shelley was fast asleep.

First Snow in the Street

I did not sleep last night.
   The falling snow was beautiful and white.
I dressed, sneaked down the stairs
And opened wide the door.
I had not seen such snow before.

Our grubby little street had gone;
The world was brand-new and everywhere
There was a pureness in the air.
I felt such peace. Watching every flake
I felt more and more awake.

I thought I'd learned all there was to know
About the trillion million different kinds
Of swirling frosty falling flakes of snow.
But that was not so.
I did not know how vividly it lit
The world with such a peaceful glow.

Upstairs my parents slept.
I could not drag myself away from that sight
To call them down and have them share
The mute miracle of the snow.
It seemed to fall for me alone.
How beautiful the grubby little street had grown!

Brian Patten

It's Winter,
It's Winter

It's winter, it's winter, it's wonderful winter,
      When everyone lounges around in the sun!

It's winter, it's winter, it's wonderful winter,
When everyone's brown like a steak overdone!

It's winter, it's winter, it's wonderful winter,
It's swimming and surfing and hunting for conkers!

It's winter, it's winter, it's wonderful winter,
And I am   completely
                    and   utterly
                                    bonkers!

KIT WRIGHT

Sledging

Look at us
As we go
Sledging on the bright white snow.

Faces beaming
Long hair streaming
Passing those who are too slow.

WENDY ELIZABETH JOHNSON

December Leaves

The fallen leaves are cornflakes
        That fill the lawn's wide dish.
And night and noon
The wind's a spoon
That stirs them with a swish.

The sky's a silver sifter
A-sifting white and slow,
That gently shakes
On crisp brown flakes
The sugar known as snow.

KAYE STARBIRD

Snowflake Soufflé

Snowflake soufflé,
        Snowflake soufflé,
Makes a lip-smacking lunch
        On an ice-cold day.

You take seven snowflakes,
        You break seven eggs,
And you stir it seven times
        With your two hind legs.

Bake it in an igloo,
        Throw it on a plate,
And slice off a slice
        With a rusty ice-skate.

X. J. Kennedy

Brown Bear's Wedding

MARTINE BECK

Brown Bear lived in the mountains, near the village of Upper Nutting. He always wore a Tyrolean hat with a long red feather in it. Brown Bear was very good at fishing. He was also very good at cooking the fish he had caught. But sometimes in the evening he felt a little sad without really knowing why.

One day, on his way to the village to do some shopping, he stopped near the frozen pond to watch the skaters. A very graceful white bear was dancing on the blue-tinged ice. She glided, spinned, and whirled, her pale pink scarf trailing in the wind. How pretty she was! Brown Bear slowly continued on his way to the market, with a smile on his face.

That evening, he tried to read *The Bears' Daily*, but his mind wasn't on it. Next day, he went back to the pond. As soon as he saw White Bear skating so gracefully, his heart beat faster. As she slid past, he caught a whiff of her delicious fir and snowdrop scent.

That night, he dreamed he was a brilliant skater and was dancing on the ice with a lovely white bear in his arms. When the sun woke him up from his beautiful dream, he felt as happy as a king bear.

First, he went outside to get some exercise. Then he took a shower, brushed his hair carefully, and dressed up in his best clothes. He walked jauntily to the frozen lake. But there was no sign of White Bear. He went all round the lake, and then all the way back again. He waited and waited, feeling sick at heart. The sky had clouded over, and the fir trees cast gloomy shadows on the path. Back home again, he simply could not get warm. He went off to sleep, a very unhappy bear.

The next day, he was so anxious about going back to the lake that he put off the moment as long as he could. But when he got there, and caught sight of White Bear's scarf, trailing in the breeze, he was overjoyed. He hired a pair of skates and dashed onto the ice . . . But down he went with a bump, flat on his face! He knew that White Bear was not far away, and he felt very ashamed and sorry for himself. But then he heard a sweet voice asking: 'Have you hurt yourself?' He looked up into White Bear's beautiful eyes and saw her lovely smile.

'No, no, not at all,' he mumbled.

She gave him her paw to help him up.

Suddenly, it began to snow heavily. 'Would you like to have a drink of hot chocolate with me?' he asked.

'That's a very good idea,' she said. 'I'm tired of skating.'

Brown Bear took her to a tea room above the village, where delicious bilberry tarts were served. White Bear's lips and paws were stained purple. They agreed to meet next day by a tall larch tree, and do some skiing together. Brown Bear zigzagged down between the fir trees, proudly showing White Bear how good he was at turning.

Another day, they climbed the snowy peaks to admire the view. Soon they were going out together every day.

'There go the two love-bears,' the villagers would say.

One evening, they saw a shooting star lighting up the sky.

'Quick, make a wish,' she murmured.

'I wish we could always be together,' he said.

She smiled.

When he got home, Brown Bear took out a sheet of paper and wrote:

Dearest and most beautiful White Bear, your eyes shine like stars and your fur is whiter than the moon. You have stolen my heart. Would you like to look at the moon and stars with me for ever and ever?

Then he slipped the letter in an envelope and told his friend Owl where to take it.

White Bear read the letter and gave Owl her pale pink scarf. Brown Bear would know what her answer was.

All their friends came to the wedding. They stood round in a circle as Brown Bear tenderly placed a crown of roses on White Bear's head, and gave her a kiss.

Everyone clapped and the celebration began. They formed a great ring and, with the music echoing in the mountains, danced away until the very last star faded in the sky.

Winter Excursions

Museums are good, when there's snow and rain.
We can see the dinosaurs again!
See them move, and hear them roar!
Everyone adores a dinosaur.

GAVIN EWART

Winter Trees

After rain,
winter trees,
like witches' brooms,
sweep the sky
clean again.

JUNE CREBBIN

The North Wind Doth Blow

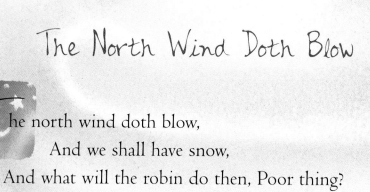

The north wind doth blow,
    And we shall have snow,
And what will the robin do then, Poor thing?
    He'll sit in a barn,
    And keep himself warm,
And hide his head under his wing, Poor thing!

The north wind doth blow,
And we shall have snow,
And what will the swallow do then, Poor thing?
    Oh, do you not know
    That he's off long ago,
To a country where he will find spring,
            Poor thing!

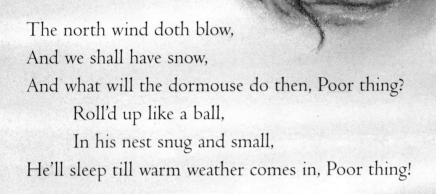

The north wind doth blow,
And we shall have snow,
And what will the dormouse do then, Poor thing?
    Roll'd up like a ball,
    In his nest snug and small,
He'll sleep till warm weather comes in, Poor thing!

The north wind doth blow,
And we shall have snow,
And what will the honey-bee do then, Poor thing?
    In his hive he will stay
    Till the cold is away,
And then he'll come out in the spring, Poor thing!

ANONYMOUS

Joe

We feed the birds in winter,
    And outside in the snow
We have a tray of many seeds
For many birds of many breeds
And one grey squirrel named Joe.
    But Joe comes early,
    Joe comes late,
    And all the birds
    Must stand and wait.
And waiting there for Joe to go
Is pretty cold work in the snow.

DAVID McCORD

Paws

My gloves are woollen paws
    My mother knitted for me
While we were watching
TV after tea.

They keep me as warm
In the winter cold
As the fur of the big white bears
Who live in the ice and snow.

STANLEY COOK

The Snowman

Mother, while you were at the shops
        and I was snoozing in my chair
I heard a tap at the window
        saw a snowman standing there

He looked so cold and miserable
        I almost could have cried
so I put the kettle on
        and invited him inside

I made him a cup of cocoa
        to warm the cockles of his nose
then he snuggled in front of the fire
        for a cosy little doze

He lay there warm and smiling
            softly counting sheep
I eavesdropped for a little while
            then I too fell asleep

            Seems he awoke and tiptoed out
                        exactly when I'm not too sure
            it's a wonder you didn't see him
                        as you came in through the door

(oh, and by the way,
the kitten's made a puddle on the floor)

            ROGER MCGOUGH

February Twilight

I stood beside a hill
    Smooth with new-laid snow,
A single star looked out
From the cold evening glow.

There was no other creature
That saw what I could see —
I stood and watched the evening star
As long as it watched me.

SARA TEASDALE